Teacher Edition
Grade 1

Getting Ready for the
Smarter Balanced
Assessment

INCLUDES

- Common Core Standards Practice in SBAC format
- Beginning-, Middle-, and End-of-Year Benchmark Tests with Performance Tasks
- Year-End Performance Assessment Task
- Student Record Forms
- Print and Digital Intervention Resources correlated to Common Core Standards

Printed in the U.S.A.

ISBN 978-0-544-25192-2

5 6 7 8 9 10   0982   22 21   20   19 18 17   16 15

4500530392   A B C D E F G

Contents

Overview of *Smarter Balanced Test Prep*

How Assessment Can Help Individualize Instruction

The *Getting Ready for the Smarter Balanced Assessment* contains different types of assessment for use throughout the school year. The following pages will explain how these assessments can be utilized to diagnose children's understanding of the Common Core State Standards and to guide instructional choices, improve children's performance, and to help facilitate their mastery of math content.

Diagnostic Assessment

Beginning-of-Year Test contains items that are presented in Common Core assessment format. This test should be utilized early in the year to establish on-grade level skills that children may already understand. This benchmark test will facilitate which customization of instructional content to optimize the time spent teaching specific objectives.

Formative Assessment

Middle-of-Year Test assesses the same standards as the Beginning-of-Year Test, allowing children's progress to be tracked and providing opportunity for instructional adjustments, when required.

Summative Assessment

End-of-Year Test assess the same standards as the Beginning- and Middle-of-Year Tests. It is the final benchmark test for the grade level. When children's performance on the End-of-Year Test is compared to performance on the Beginning- and Middle-of-Year Tests, teachers are able to document children's growth.

Performance Assessment Tasks are provided for each Benchmark Test and as a Year-End Performance Assessment. Each assessment contains several tasks to assess children's ability to use what they have learned and provides an opportunity for children to display their thinking strategies. Each set of tasks is accompanied by teacher support pages and a rubric for scoring.

Performance Assessment

Performance Assessment, together with other types of assessment, can supply the missing information not provided by other testing formats. Performance Assessments, in particular, help reveal the thinking strategies children use to work through a problem. Performance Assessments with multiple tasks for each Benchmark Test and a Year-End Performance Assessment are provided in the *Getting Ready for the Smarter Balanced Assessment*.

Each of these assessments has several tasks that target specific math concepts, skills, and strategies. These tasks can help assess children's ability to use what they have learned to solve everyday problems. Each assessment focuses on a theme. Teachers can plan for children to complete one task at a time or use an extended amount of time to complete the entire assessment.

Teacher support pages introduce each Performance Assessment. These are followed by the tasks for the children. A task-specific rubric helps teachers evaluate children's work.

Resources

Intervention Resources

For skills that children have not yet mastered, the Intervention Resources provide prescriptive information for additional instruction and practice on concepts and skills. Intervention Resources are correlated for each Common Core Standard.

Using Student and Class Record Forms

The *Getting Ready for the Smarter Balanced Assessment* includes Student and Class Record Forms. On the Student Record Form, each test item is correlated to the standard it assesses. These forms can be used to:

- Follow progress throughout the year.
- Identify strengths, weaknesses, and provide follow-up instruction.
- Make assignments based on the intervention options provided.

Common Core Assessment Formats

Common Core Assessment consortia have developed assessments that contain item types beyond the traditional multiple-choice format. This allows for a more robust assessment of children's understanding of concepts. Common Core assessments will be administered via computers; and *Getting Ready for the Smarter Balanced Assessment* presents items in formats similar to what children will see on the tests. The following information is provided to help teachers familiarize children with these different types of items. Each item type is identified on pages (ix–x). You may want to use the examples to introduce the item types to children. The following explanations are provided to guide children in answering the questions. These pages describe the most common item types. You may find other types on some tests.

Example 1 Tell if a number matches another representation.

Yes or No

For this type of item, children respond to a single question with for several examples. There will be a question and children will fill in the bubble next to "Yes" or "No" to answer for each part. They must fill in a bubble for each part.

Example 2 Choose numbers less than a given number.

More Than One Correct Choice

This type of item may confuse children because it looks like a traditional multiple-choice item. Tell children this type of item will ask them to choose all of something. Explain that when the item asks them to find all, they should look for more than one correct choice. Tell them to carefully look at each choice and mark it if it is a correct answer.

Example 3 Choose tens and ones to describe a number.

Choose From a List

Sometimes when children take a test on a computer, they will have to select a word, number, or symbol from a drop-down list. The *Getting Ready for the Smarter Balanced Assessment* tests show a list and ask children to choose the correct answer. Tell children to make their choice by circling the correct answer. There will only be one choice that is correct.

Example 4 Sort numbers into groups for greater than or less than a given number.

Sorting

Children may be asked to sort something into categories. These items will present numbers, words, or equations on rectangular "tiles." The directions will ask children to write each of the items in the box that tells about. Tell children that sometimes they may write the same number or word in more than one box. For example, if they need to sort quadrilaterals by category, a square could be in a box labeled rectangle and another box labeled rhombus.

Example 5 Order numbers from least to greatest.

Use Given Numbers in the Answer

Children may also see numbers and symbols on tiles when they are asked to write an equation or answer a question using only numbers. They should use the given numbers to write the answer to the problem. Sometimes there will be extra numbers. They may also need to use each number more than once.

Example 6 Match related facts.

Matching

Some items will ask children to match equivalent values or other related items. The directions will specify what they should match. There will be dots to guide them in drawing lines. The matching may be between columns or rows.

Example 1

Yes or No

Fill in a bubble for each part.

1. Is it another way to show 42?
Choose Yes or No.

40 + 2	● Yes	○ No
	○ Yes	● No
4 + 2	○ Yes	● No
‖‖‖ ° °	● Yes	○ No

Example 2

More Than One Correct Choice

Fill in the bubble next to all the correct answers.

2. Choose all the numbers less than 25.

○ 32

● 24

○ 52

● 17

○ 61

Example 3

Choose From a List

Circle the words.

3. What is another way to write 24?

2 | (tens) / ones | 4 | tens / (ones)

Example 4

Sorting

Copy the numbers in the right box.

4. Write each number in the box that tells about it.

33	46	72	97

Less than 50	Greater than 50
33 46	72 97

Example 5

Use the Numbers

Write the numbers.

5. Write the numbers in order from least to greatest.

18	12	21	8

8   12   18   21

Example 6

Matching

Draw lines to match.

6. Match the related facts.

$3 + 2 = 5$ $9 - 6 = 3$

$8 - 2 = 6$ $2 + 3 = 5$

$3 + 6 = 9$ $2 + 7 = 9$

$9 - 7 = 2$ $8 - 6 = 2$

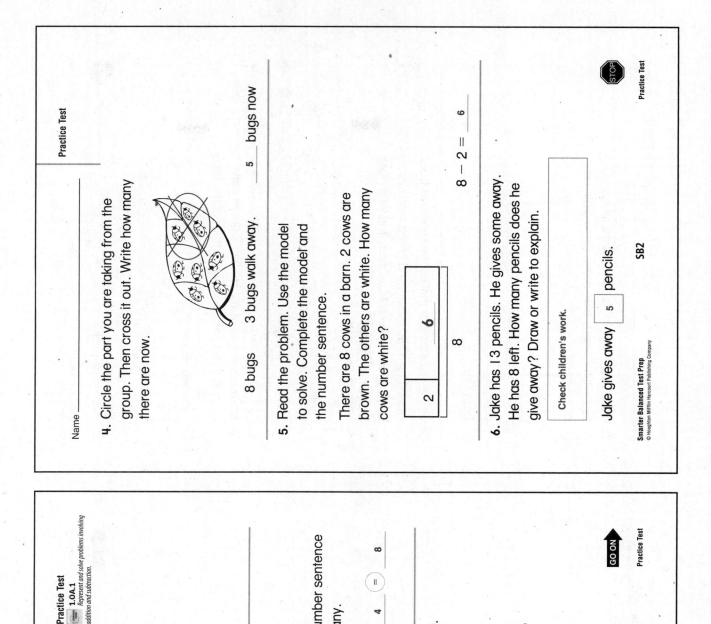

Name _____

4. Circle the part you are taking from the group. Then cross it out. Write how many there are now.

8 bugs   3 bugs walk away.   __5__ bugs now

5. Read the problem. Use the model to solve. Complete the model and the number sentence.

There are 8 cows in a barn. 2 cows are brown. The others are white. How many cows are white?

2	6

8

$8 - 2 = 6$

6. Jake has 13 pencils. He gives some away. He has 8 left. How many pencils does he give away? Draw or write to explain.

Check children's work.

Jake gives away [5] pencils.

Name _____

1. Write the addition problem.

4		2

$+$

6

2. There are 4 red leaves and 4 yellow leaves. How many leaves are there?

Draw to show your work.

Write the number sentence and how many.

4 + 4 = 8

3. James has 5 marbles. He finds more marbles. Then he has 9 marbles. How many marbles does James find?

5	4

9

5 + __4__ = 9

Name _____

1.O.A.2
Represent and solve problems involving
addition and subtraction.

1. Ted has 7 red apples. He has 3 yellow apples. He has 2 green apples. Draw a picture of the apples.

Check children's drawings.

Ted has [12] apples.

2. Jude has 8 green blocks, 4 red blocks, and 2 green blocks. How many blocks does Jude have?

[14]
_____ blocks
label

3. Paula has 6 red flowers. She has 4 pink flowers. She has 7 yellow flowers. Draw a picture of the flowers.

Check children's drawings.

Paula has [17] flowers.

Name _____

4. Beth sees 4 red birds. She sees 2 yellow birds. She sees 4 blue birds. Draw a picture of the birds.

Drawings will vary.

Beth sees [10] birds.

Circle the number that makes the sentence true.

5. David has 6 red markers, 5 green markers, and 7 blue markers. How many markers does David have in all?

David has | 11 | 12 | (18) | markers.

6. Enzo has 5 blue pens. He has 4 green pens. He has 5 red pens. Draw a picture of the pens.

Drawings will vary.

Enzo has [14] pens.

Name _____

4. Write the addends in a different order.

2 + 5 = 7

_5_ + _2_ = 7

5. Look at the [cubes]. Complete the addition sentence to show the sum. Choose the missing number and the sum.

3 + ⟨6⟩ = | 2 | ⑥ | 8 |

___ + 2 = | 9 | 10 | ⑪ |

6. Write two ways to group and add 3 + 6 + 1.

9 + 1 = 10

3 + 7 = 10

Name _____

1.OA.3 *Understand and apply properties of operations and the relationship between addition and subtraction.*

1. Choose all the pictures that show adding zero.

2. Draw lines to match addition sentences with the same addends in a different order.

4 + 3 = 7   2 + 4 = 6   3 + 6 = 9

4 + 2 = 6   6 + 3 = 9   3 + 4 = 7

3. Draw a model to show that 5 + 3 is the same as 3 + 5. Show how you know.

Drawings should show that combining 5 and 3 in any order makes 8. Children may compare the lengths of cube trains or show one-to-one correspondence to prove equality.

GO ON

Name ___

Practice Test
1.OA.4 Understand and apply properties of operations and the relationship between addition and subtraction.

1. Look at the facts. A number is missing. Which number is missing?

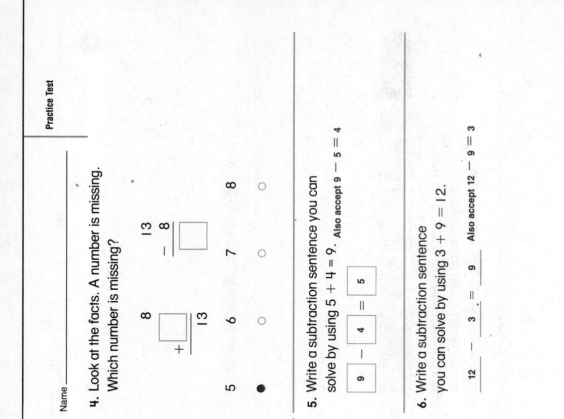

$$7 + \boxed{} = 13$$
$$13 - 7 = \boxed{} \; 8$$

○ 5   ● 6   ○ 7   ○ 8

2. Write a subtraction sentence you can solve by using 4 + 2 = 6.

$$6 - \boxed{4} = \boxed{2}$$ Also accept $$6 - \boxed{2} = \boxed{4}$$

3. Look at the facts. Write the missing number in each fact.

$$\boxed{7} + 5 = 12$$
$$12 - 5 = \boxed{7}$$

4. Look at the facts. A number is missing. Which number is missing?

$$8 + \boxed{} = 13$$
$$13 - 8 = \boxed{}$$

● 5   ○ 6   ○ 7   ○ 8

5. Write a subtraction sentence you can solve by using 5 + 4 = 9.

$$9 - \boxed{4} = \boxed{5}$$ Also accept $9 - 5 = 4$.

6. Write a subtraction sentence you can solve by using 3 + 9 = 12.

$$12 - \boxed{3} = \boxed{9}$$ Also accept $12 - 9 = 3$.

Smarter Balanced Test Prep
© Houghton Mifflin Harcourt Publishing Company
SB7

Smarter Balanced Test Prep
© Houghton Mifflin Harcourt Publishing Company
SB8

Practice Test

GO ON   STOP

Name _____

4. Count on from 4. Write the number that shows 1 more.

_____ 5

5. Count back. Write the number that is 2 less.

8 – 2 = 6

6. ☆ means "count back 1."
▢ means "count back 2."
● means "count back 3."
Match each picture to a number sentence.

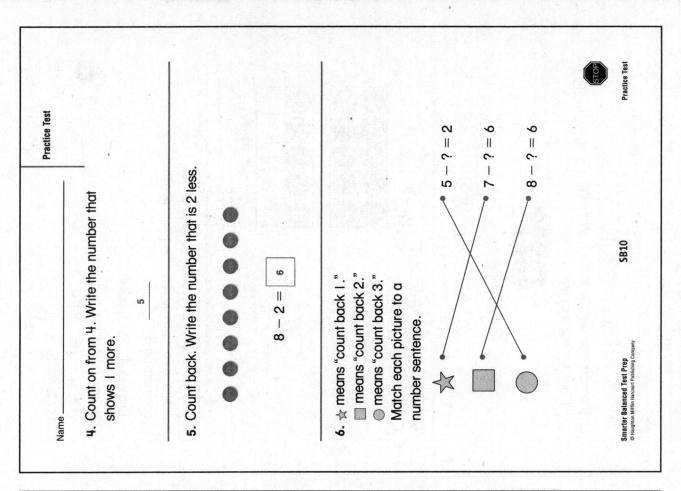

5 – ? = 2
7 – ? = 6
8 – ? = 6

Smarter Balanced Test Prep
© Houghton Mifflin Harcourt Publishing Company

Practice Test
1.OA.5
Add and subtract within 20.

Name _____

1. Count on from 6. Write the number that shows 2 more.

_____ 8

2. Count back. Write the number that is 1 less.

6 – 1 = 5

3. ☆ means "count back 1."
▢ means "count back 2."
● means "count back 3."
Match each picture to a number sentence.

8 – ? = 6
6 – ? = 3
11 – ? = 10

Smarter Balanced Test Prep
© Houghton Mifflin Harcourt Publishing Company

GO ON
Practice Test

STOP
Practice Test

Smarter Balanced Test Prep
© Houghton Mifflin Harcourt Publishing Company

SB9–SB10

Answer Key

Name ____________

Practice Test

1.OA.6 *Add and subtract within 20.*

1. Write the subtraction sentence the picture shows.

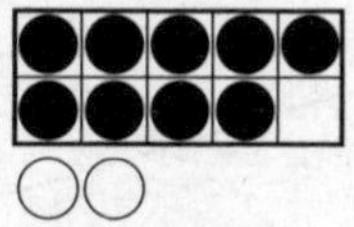

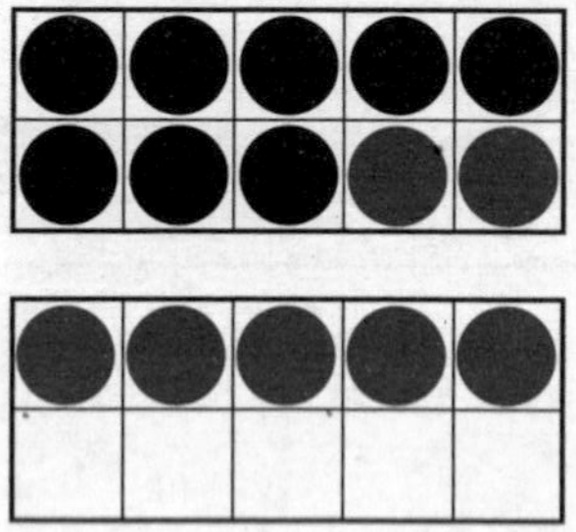

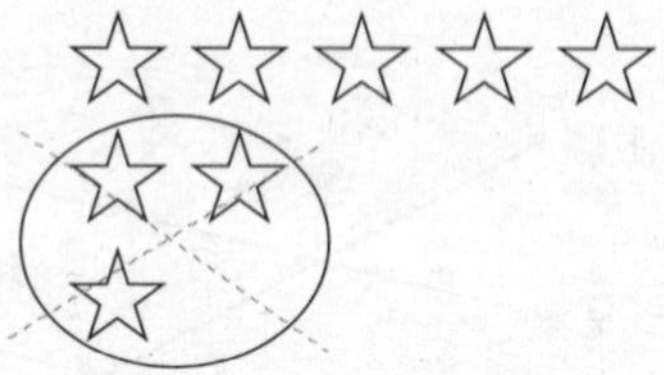

8 − 3 = 5

Explain.

Possible answer: I take 3 stars from the group of 8 stars.

There are 5 stars left.

2. Write a count on 2 fact to show a sum of 6. Then write a doubles fact to show a sum of 6.

4 + 2 = 6; 3 + 3 = 6

GO ON

Name ____________

Practice Test

3. The model shows 9 + 2 = 11. Write the 10 fact that has the same sum.

10 + 1 = 11

4. Make a ten to subtract.
Draw to show your work.
Write the difference.

15 − 8 = ?

15 − 8 = 7

5. Tina has a book. She reads 10 pages. Then she reads 6 more pages. How many pages does she read?

Tina reads **16** pages.

Write a related fact to check.

16 − **6** = 10

STOP

Name _____

6. Is the math sentence true? Choose Yes or No.

$6 + 3 = 3 + 6$	● Yes ○ No
$10 = 6 + 4$	● Yes ○ No
$5 + 2 = 4 - 3$	○ Yes ● No

7. Which are true? Use a ✏ to color.

20 = 20	9 + 1 + 1 = 11	8 − 0 = 8
12 = 1 + 2	10 + 1 = 1 + 10	7 = 14 + 7
	6 = 2 + 2 + 2	
	11 − 5 = 1 + 5	
	1 + 2 + 3 = 4 + 5	

8. Is the math sentence true? Choose Yes or No.

$7 + 2 = 9 - 2$	○ Yes ● No
$9 = 6 + 3$	● Yes ○ No
$5 + 4 = 4 + 5$	● Yes ○ No

1.OA.7 *Work with addition and subtraction equations.*

Name _____

Which are true? Circle your answers.
Which are false? Cross out your answers.

1. (1 + 9 = 9) (8 + 1 = 2 + 7) (19 = 19)

2. (8 = 5 + 3) (8 + 5 = 5 + 8) (6 + 2 = 4 + 4)

3. (9 + 7 = 16) (16 − 9 = 9 + 7) (9 − 7 = 7 + 9)

4. (12 − 3 = 9 − 0) (11 = 1 + 5 + 5) (10 − 8 = 2)

5. Is the math sentence true? Circle Yes or No.

$5 - 4 = 9 - 8$	● Yes ○ No
$13 = 5 + 7$	○ Yes ● No
$6 + 2 = 2 + 6$	● Yes ○ No

GO ON

Name _____

Practice Test
1.OA.8 *Work with addition and subtraction equations.*

1. Look at the picture. How many fewer plates are there than cups? Choose the number.

| 8 |
| 5 |
| (2) |

fewer plates

2. Use 🔲, to find the unknown numbers. Write the numbers.

$7 + \underline{5} = 12$

$12 - 7 = \underline{5}$

3. Which is the unknown number in these related facts?

$\underline{} + 3 = 11 \qquad 11 - 3 = \underline{}$

$3 + \underline{} = 11 \qquad 11 - \underline{} = 3$

○ 1   ○ 3   ● 8   ○ 9

SB15

GO ON

Practice Test

Name _____

4. Look at the number sentences. What number is missing? Write the number in each box.

$13 - \boxed{4} = 9 \qquad 9 + \boxed{4} = 13$

5. Use 🔲, to find the unknown numbers. Write the numbers.

$6 + \underline{10} = 16$

$16 - 6 = \underline{10}$

6. Which is the unknown number in these related facts?

$\underline{} + 4 = 13 \qquad 13 - 4 = \underline{}$

$4 + \underline{} = 13 \qquad 13 - \underline{} = 4$

○ 5   ○ 7   ○ 8   ● 9

SB16

STOP

Practice Test

1. Lucy counts 38 cubes. Then she counts forward some more cubes. Write the numbers.

38, | 39 | , | 40 | , | 41 | , | 42 | , | 43 | , | 44 |

2. Match each number on the left to a number that is 10 more.

25 — 45
39 — 29
79 — 15
55 — 69

3. What number does the model show?

_____ 103

---

4. Felix counts 46 cubes. Then he counts forward some more cubes. Write the numbers.

46, | 47 | , | 48 | , | 49 | , | 50 | , | 51 | , | 52 |

5. Count by tens. Match each number on the left to a number that is 10 more.

69 — 59
59 — 65
75 — 49
45 — 35
67 — 57

6. What number does the model show?

_____ 110

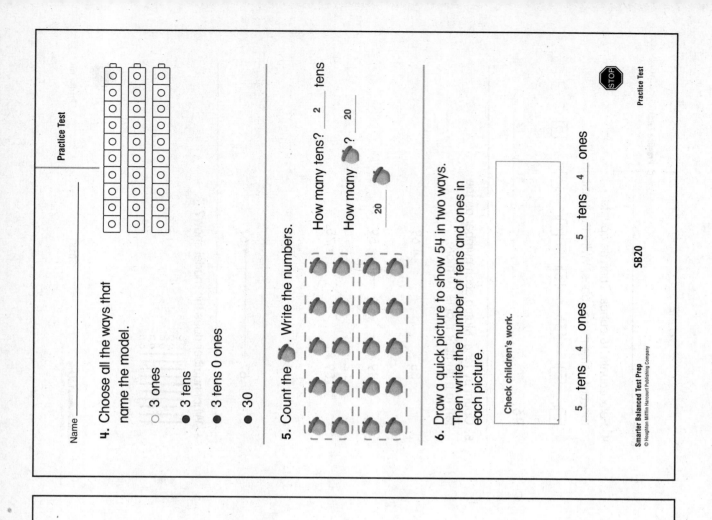

Name _____

4. Choose all the ways that name the model.

○ 3 ones

● 3 tens

● 3 tens 0 ones

● 30

5. Count the 🍓. Write the numbers.

How many tens? __2__ tens

How many 🍓 ? __20__

__20__

6. Draw a quick picture to show 54 in two ways. Then write the number of tens and ones in each picture.

Check children's work.

__5__ tens __4__ ones   __5__ tens __4__ ones

STOP

Name _____

I. Choose all the ways that name the model.

● 70

● 7 tens

● 7 tens 0 ones

○ 7 ones

2. Count the 🦃. Write the numbers.

How many tens? __3__ tens

How many 🦃 ? __30__

🦃

3. Draw a quick picture to show 42 in two ways. Then write the number of tens and ones in each picture.

Check children's work.

__4__ tens __2__ ones   __4__ tens __2__ ones

1.NBT.2B
Understand place value.

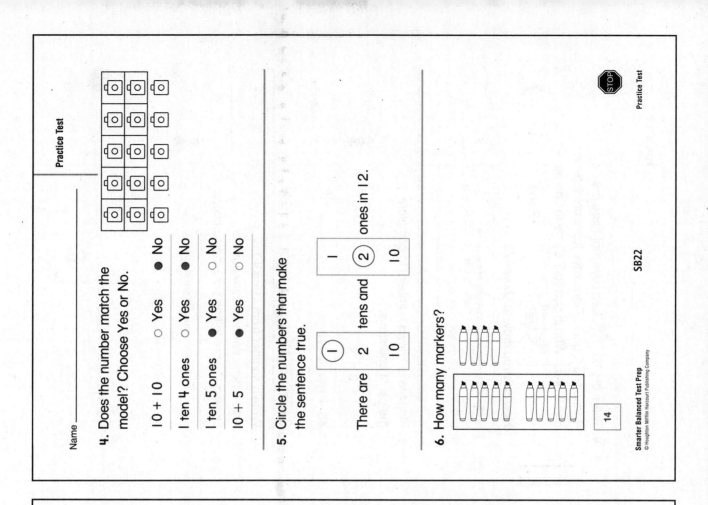

Name _____

1. Does the number match the model? Choose Yes or No.

1 ten and 3 ones	○ Yes	● No
1 ten and 6 ones	● Yes	○ No
10 + 5	○ Yes	● No
10 + 6	● Yes	○ No

2. Circle the numbers that make the sentence true.

There are [10 | 5 | (1)] tens and [10 | (5) | 1] ones in 15.

Draw 10-sticks and circles.
Write how many tens and ones.

3. 13

○ ○ ○

[1] tens [3] ones = 13

Name _____

4. Does the number match the model? Choose Yes or No.

10 + 10	○ Yes	● No
1 ten 4 ones	○ Yes	● No
1 ten 5 ones	● Yes	○ No
10 + 5	● Yes	○ No

5. Circle the numbers that make the sentence true.

There are [(1) | 2 | 10] tens and [1 | (2) | 10] ones in 12.

6. How many markers?

[14]

1. There are 27 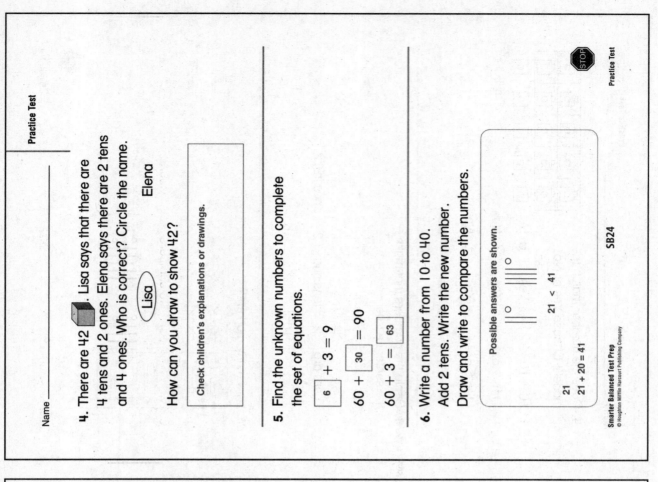. Dave says that there are 7 tens and 2 ones. Kara says there are 2 tens and 7 ones. Who is correct? Circle the name.

Dave   (Kara)

How can you draw to show 27?

Check children's explanations or drawings.

2. Find the unknown numbers to complete the set of equations.

$3 + \boxed{7} = 10$

$30 + 70 = \boxed{100}$

$30 + \boxed{7} = 37$

3. Choose all the ways that name the model.

● 90
● 9 tens
● 9 tens 0 ones
○ 9 ones

---

4. There are 42 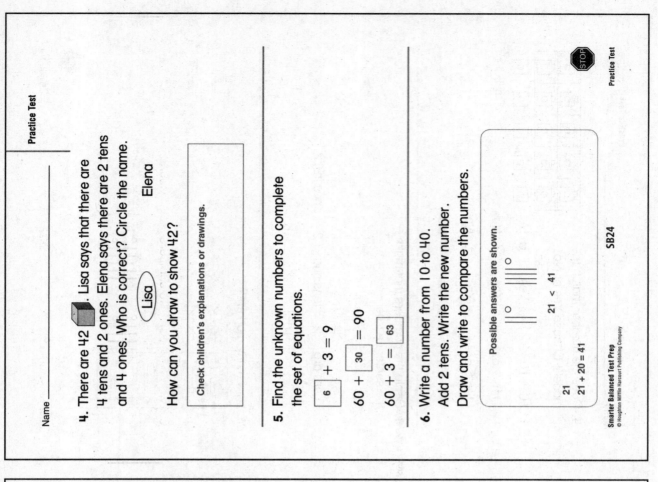. Lisa says that there are 4 tens and 2 ones. Elena says there are 2 tens and 4 ones. Who is correct? Circle the name.

(Lisa)   Elena

How can you draw to show 42?

Check children's explanations or drawings.

5. Find the unknown numbers to complete the set of equations.

$\boxed{6} + 3 = 9$

$60 + \boxed{30} = 90$

$60 + 3 = \boxed{63}$

6. Write a number from 10 to 40. Add 2 tens. Write the new number. Draw and write to compare the numbers.

Possible answers are shown.

21

21 + 20 = 41

21 < 41

Name _____

1.NBT.3
Understand place value.

1. Compare. Is the math sentence true? Choose Yes or No.

39 is greater than 43. ○ Yes ● No

71 is greater than 35. ● Yes ○ No

49 < 20 ○ Yes ● No

75 > 25 ● Yes ○ No

2. Choose all the numbers that are less than 51.

● 41

● 48

○ 75

● 37

3. Circle the symbol that makes the math sentence true.

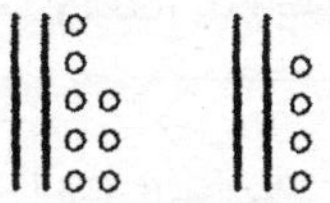

28 [○○○○ / ○○○○] 24

(>) < =

Name _____

4. Greg has these number cards. Write each number in the box to show **less than 61** or **greater than 61**.

64 59 68 69 60

less than 61	greater than 61
59	64
60	68
	69

5. Choose all the math sentences that are true.

○ 27 > 31

● 35 = 35

● 71 < 77

○ 82 < 70

● 64 > 46

6. Write <, >, or = to compare the numbers.

46 < 58

Practice Test

1.NBT.4

Use place value understanding and properties of operations to add and subtract.

1. Choose all the ways that name the model.

_____
_____
_____
_____
_____
_____
_____

○ 9
● 2 tens and 7 tens
● 20 + 70
● 90

2. Use the model. Draw to show how to add the ones.

24 + 3 = 27

Check children's drawings. Possible drawing shown.

3. Use the model. Draw to show how to make a ten.

37 + 6 = 43

Check children's drawings. Possible drawing shown.

---

4. Write the addition sentence that the model shows. Solve.

Tens	Ones

32 + 41 = 73

5. What is the sum?

$$\begin{array}{r} 30 \\ +40 \\ \hline \end{array}$$

○ 20
○ 50
● 70
○ 80

6. Gina has 14 pennies. Her brother gives her 23 more. How many pennies does Gina have? Circle the number that makes the sentence true.

Gina has ⟨37⟩ 34 33 pennies.

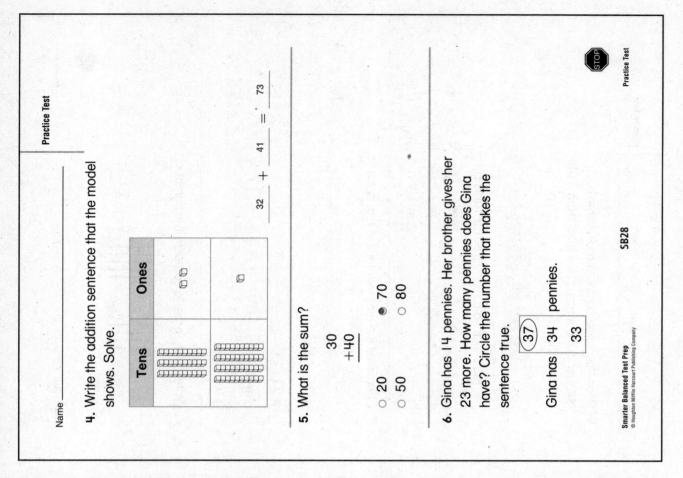

4. Use mental math. Complete the chart.

10 Less		10 More
23	33	43
47	57	67

5. Draw a quick picture to show a number that is 10 more than the model.

6. Use mental math. Write the numbers that are 10 less and 10 more.

| 27 | 37 | 47 |

---

1. Use mental math. Complete the chart.

10 Less		10 More
12	22	32
35	45	55

2. Draw a quick picture to show a number that is 10 less than the model.

3. Use mental math. Write the numbers that are 10 less and 10 more.

| 14 | 24 | 34 |

Name _____

1. Bruno has 90 shirts in his store. He sells 40 of them. How many shirts are left? Show your work.

1.NBT.6 Use place value understanding and properties of operations to add and subtract.

___50___ shirts

2. Match the math sentences that count up and back by tens.

47 + 40 = ?   57 + 30 = ?   46 + 10 = ?

56 − 10 = ?   87 − 40 = ?   87 − 30 = ?

3. Find the sum of 20 and 32. Use any way to add.

20 + 32 = ___52___

Explain how you solved the problem.

Check children's answers. Possible answer: 20 has no ones. I added tens.

Name _____

4. Sasha has 70 stickers. She uses 40 of them. How many stickers are left? Show your work.

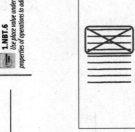

___30___ stickers

5. Match the math sentences that count up and back by tens.

38 + 30 = ?   48 + 40 = ?   38 + 20 = ?

58 − 20 = ?   68 − 30 = ?   88 − 40 = ?

6. Find the sum of 62 and 15. Use any way to add.

62 + 15 = ___77___

Explain how you solved the problem.

Check children's answers. Possible answer: I do not need to make a ten. I can add tens and ones.

Name _____

4. Match each word on the left to a drawing on the right.

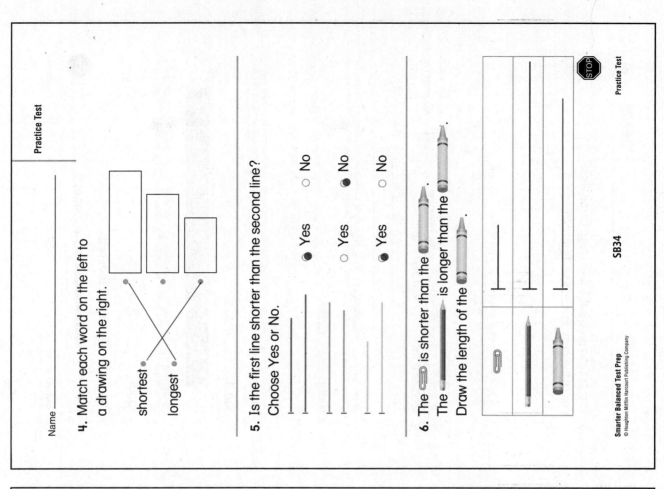

shortest

longest

5. Is the first line shorter than the second line? Choose Yes or No.

○ Yes   ○ No

● Yes   ○ No

○ Yes   ● No

● Yes   ○ No

6. The 📎 is shorter than the ___.

The ___ is longer than the ___.

Draw the length of the ___.

Name _____

1. Match each word on the left to a drawing on the right.

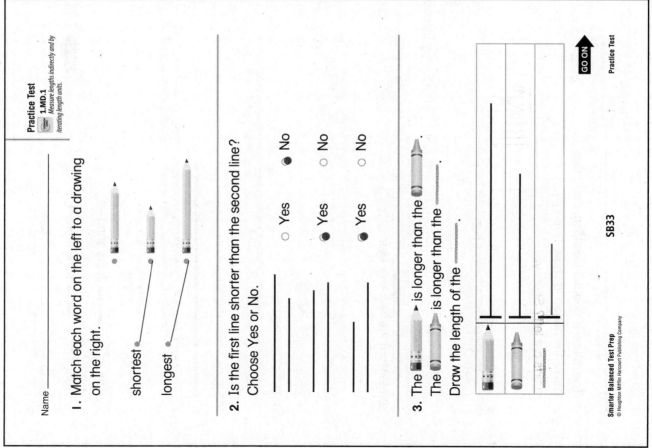

shortest

longest

2. Is the first line shorter than the second line? Choose Yes or No.

○ Yes   ● No

● Yes   ○ No

● Yes   ○ No

3. The ___ is longer than the ___.

The ___ is longer than the ___.

Draw the length of the ___.

Name _____

3. The crayon is about 5 tiles long. Draw tiles below the crayon to show its length.

Check children's drawings for 5 square tiles that show the length of the crayon.

4. Measure the ▬. Use 📎 .

about 3

about 1

about 5

The gray is the shortest.

The black is the longest.

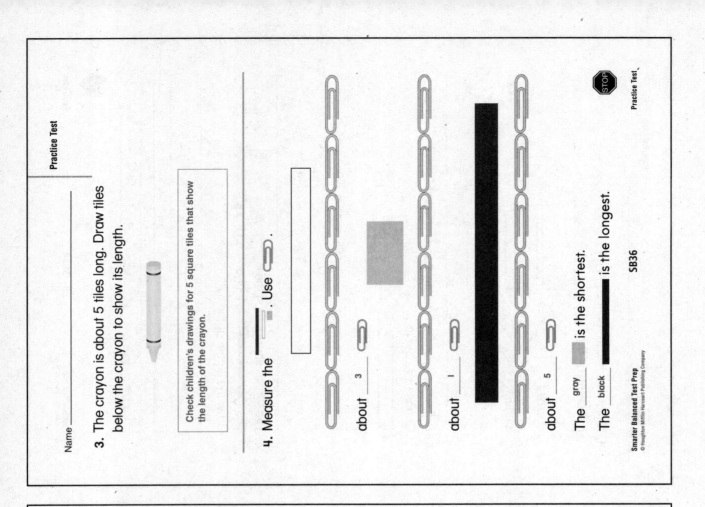

Practice Test
1.MD.2 Measure lengths indirectly and by iterating length units.

Name _____

1. The ribbon is about 3 tiles long. Draw tiles below the ribbon to show its length.

Check children's drawings for 3 square tiles that show the length of the ribbon.

2. Measure the ▬. Use 📎 .

about 3

about 2

about 4

The gray is the shortest.

The black is the longest.

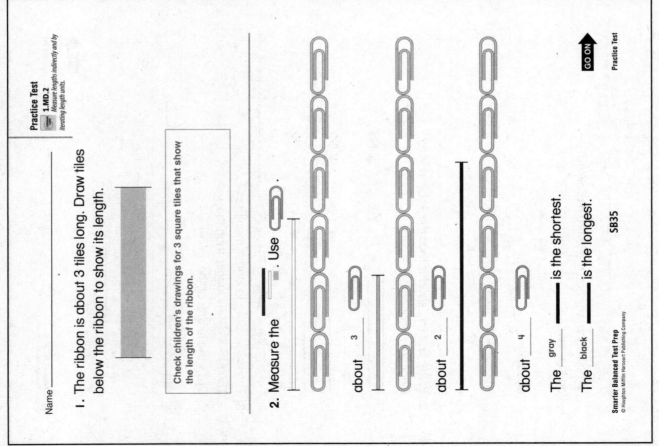

Name _____

4. Dan tried to show 4:00.
He made a mistake.

Draw hands on the
clock to show 4:00.

What did Dan do wrong? Explain Dan's mistake.

He forgot to draw a hand. He did not draw the minute
hand.

5. Look at the hour hand. What is the time?

○ 9:00
● 10 o'clock
○ 11 o'clock
○ 12:00

6. Draw the hand on the clock to show 9:30.

minute hand in the clock face pointing to 6

Name _____

1. Look at the hour hand. What is the time?

○ 2:00
○ 3 o'clock
● 4 o'clock
○ 5:00

2. What time is it? Circle the time that makes the sentence true.

The time is   2:30   3:00   3:30

3. Draw a hand on the clock to show 3:00.

minute hand in the clock face pointing to 12

Name _____

Toys at the Store

Use the bar graph to answer the questions.

Kind of Toys							
🪀 yo-yo							
🧸 doll							
〰 jump rope							
	0	1	2	3	4	5	6

Number of Toys

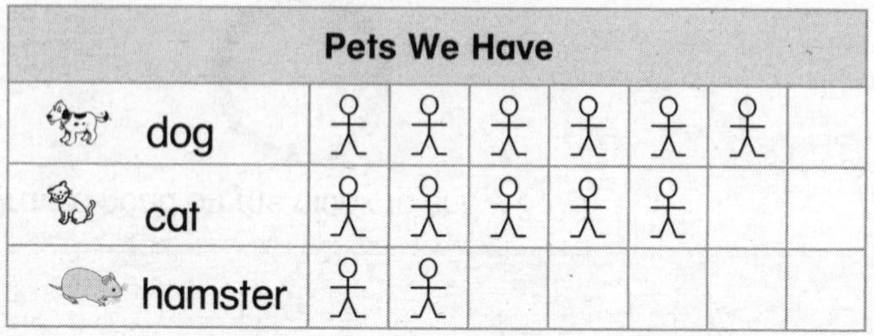

4. How many 🧸 does the store have?

[3]

---

5. Compare 🪀 and 🧸. Circle the number that makes the sentence true.

There are | 1 |
| 2 | more 🪀 than 🧸.
| ③ |

---

6. Jason says the graph shows 2 more yo-yos than dolls. Is he correct? Choose Yes or No.

● Yes   ○ No

Explain your answer.

Possible answer: There are 2 more yo-yos than dolls.

🛑 STOP   **Practice Test**

Name _____

Use the picture graph to answer the questions.

Pets We Have

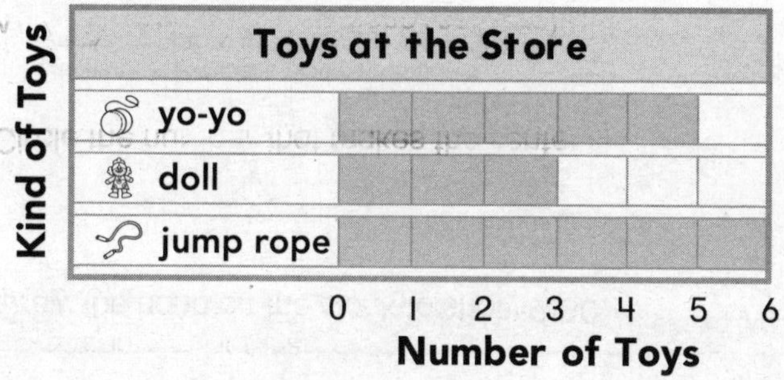

🐕 dog	太	太	太	太	太	太
🐈 cat	太	太	太	太		
🐹 hamster	太	太				

Each 太 stands for 1 child

1. How many children have 🐕 ?

[5]

---

2. Is the sentence true? Choose Yes or No.

More children have dogs than cats.   ● Yes   ○ No

6 children have dogs.   ● Yes   ○ No

2 more children have hamsters than cats.   ○ Yes   ● No

---

3. 1 more child gets a 🐹 . Draw what the hamster row looks like now.

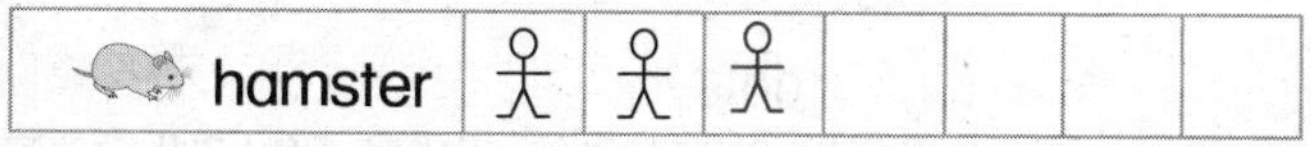

🐹 hamster	太	太	太			

⬆ GO ON   **Practice Test**

Name _____

1.G.1
Reason with shapes and their attributes.

1. Match each shape to the group where it belongs.

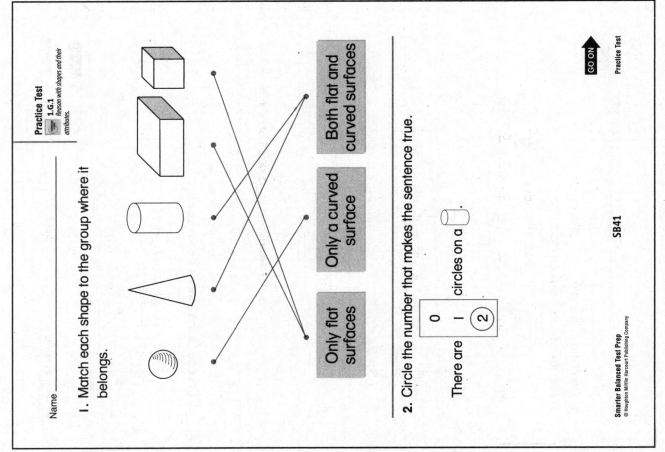

Only flat surfaces

Only a curved surface

Both flat and curved surfaces

2. Circle the number that makes the sentence true.

There are | 0 | 1 | ② circles on a ⬜.

Name _____

3. Adela wants to trace a ⬛. She finds these objects.

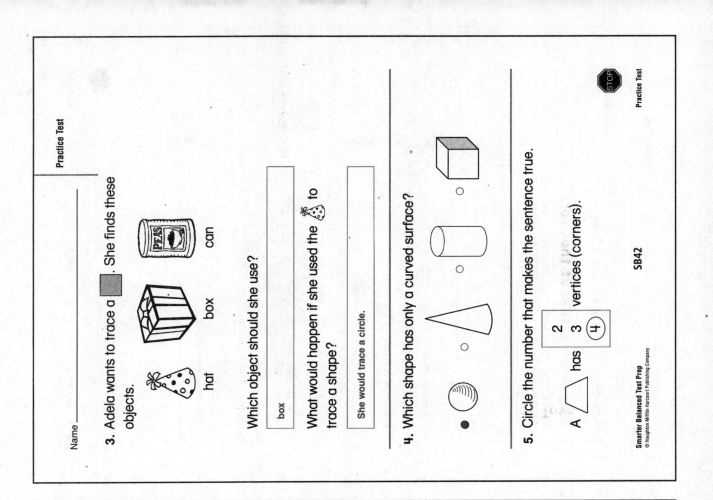

hat · box · can

Which object should she use?

box

What would happen if she used the 🎉 to trace a shape?

She would trace a circle.

4. Which shape has only a curved surface?

5. Circle the number that makes the sentence true.

A ◺ has | 2 | 3 | ④ vertices (corners).

Name _____

3. How many △ make a △ ?

Use pattern blocks. Draw to show the blocks you used.
Possible drawing shown. Orientation of drawing may vary.

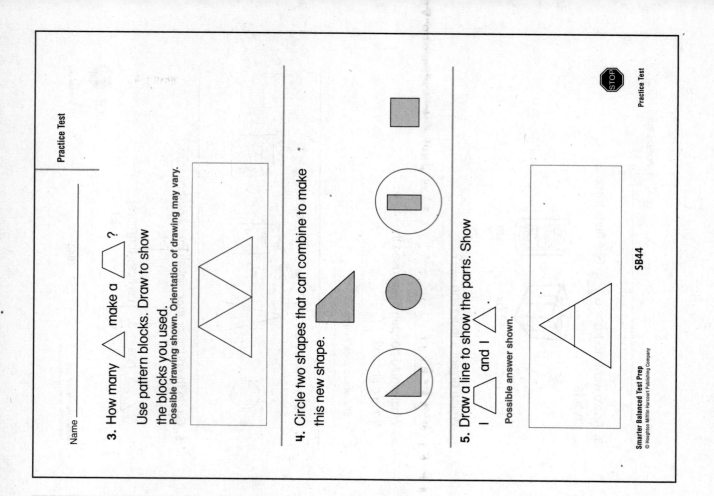

4. Circle two shapes that can combine to make this new shape.

5. Draw a line to show the parts. Show ▷ and I △.
Possible answer shown.

SB44

Smarter Balanced Test Prep
© Houghton Mifflin Harcourt Publishing Company

Name _____

I. Combine ▱ and ▱. Choose all the new shapes you can make.

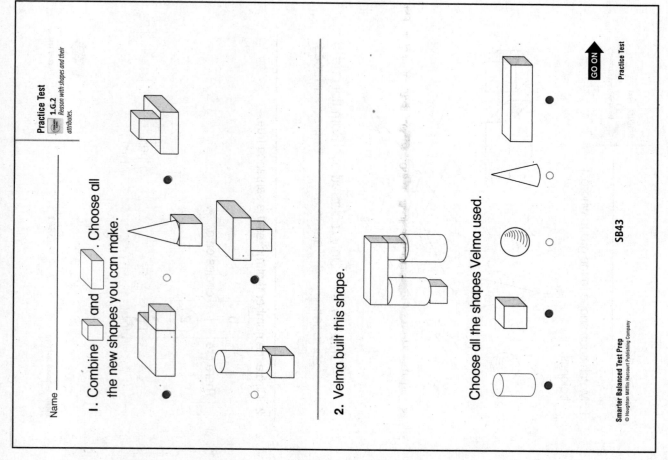

2. Velma built this shape.

Choose all the shapes Velma used.

SB43

GO ON →

Smarter Balanced Test Prep
© Houghton Mifflin Harcourt Publishing Company

Name _____

3. Circle the shapes that show halves.

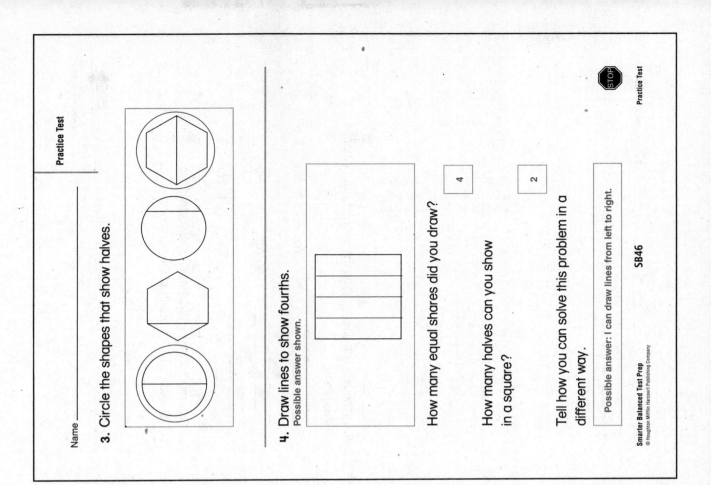

4. Draw lines to show fourths.
Possible answer shown.

How many equal shares did you draw? [4]

How many halves can you show in a square? [2]

Tell how you can solve this problem in a different way.

Possible answer: I can draw lines from left to right.

Smarter Balanced Test Prep
© Houghton Mifflin Harcourt Publishing Company

Name _____

1.G.3 Reason with shapes and their attributes.

1. Does the shape show equal shares? Choose Yes or No.

○ Yes   ● No

● Yes   ○ No

● Yes   ○ No

2. Does this shape show equal shares? Choose Yes or No.

● Yes   ○ No

○ Yes   ● No

● Yes   ○ No

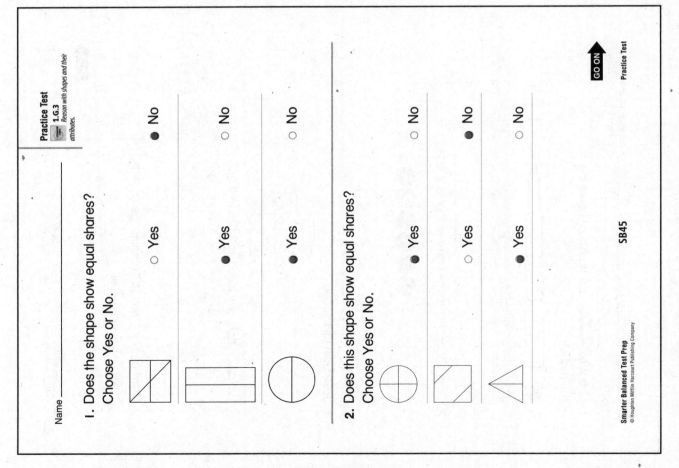

GO ON · Practice Test

Smarter Balanced Test Prep
© Houghton Mifflin Harcourt Publishing Company

Name _____

4. Choose all the ways that show the same number.

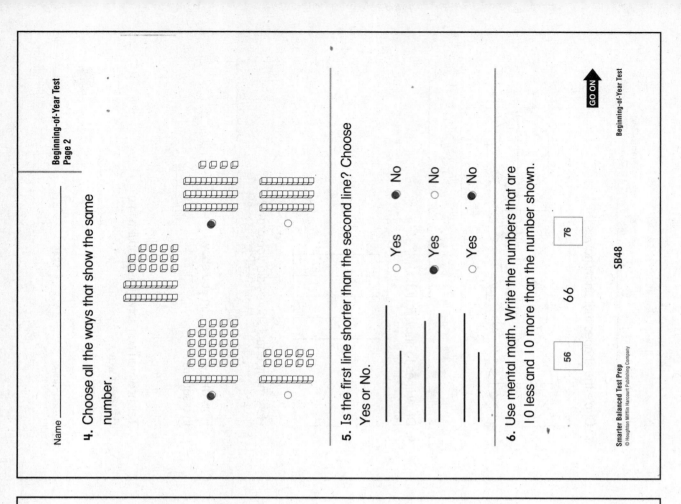

5. Is the first line shorter than the second line? Choose Yes or No.

○ Yes   ● No

● Yes   ○ No

○ Yes   ● No

6. Use mental math. Write the numbers that are 10 less and 10 more than the number shown.

| 56 | 66 | 76 |

GO ON →

Name _____

1. Use the ⌷ below. About how long is the marker?

about __4__

2. Count back. Write the number that is 2 less.

6 − 2 = 4

3. José built this shape.

Which objects did José use? Circle them.

Draw another way to combine the objects.

Check children's drawings.

GO ON →

Name _____

10. Draw a line to show one half. Color one half of the shape.

Possible answer is shown.

11. Read the problem. Write a number to solve.

I am greater than 36.
I am less than 40.
I have 8 ones.

38

12. Zeke has 60 books. He gives away 20 of them. How many books does he have now? Show your work.

40 books

Name _____

7. Look at the number sentences. What number is missing? Write the number in each box.

$15 - \boxed{6} = 9$ $9 + \boxed{6} = 15$

8. Use the hundred chart to add. Count on by ones or tens.

1	2	3	4	5	6	7	8	9	10
11	12	13	14	15	16	17	18	19	20
21	22	23	24	25	26	27	28	29	30
31	32	33	34	35	36	37	38	39	40
41	42	43	44	45	46	47	48	49	50
51	52	53	54	55	56	57	58	59	60
61	62	63	64	65	66	67	68	69	70
71	72	73	74	75	76	77	78	79	80
81	82	83	84	85	86	87	88	89	90
91	92	93	94	95	96	97	98	99	100

$54 + 20 = \underline{74}$

Explain how you used the chart to find the sum.

Possible answer: I start at 54. I count on 2 tens.

9. Chet has 13 shells. He gives 6 away. How many does he have left?

6 | 7

13

7 shells left

16. Look at the facts. A number is missing.
Which number is missing?

$$7 + \boxed{} = 15$$

$$15 - 7 = \boxed{}$$

○ 5
○ 6
○ 7
● 8

17. Finish the drawing to show 115.

Write to explain.

Possible answer: I drew two more tens to show 115.

18. Circle the numbers that make the sentence true.

There are | 10 | 6 | (1) | tens and | 10 | (6) | 1 | ones in 16.

---

13. Choose all the ways that name the time
on the clock.

● 8:30
○ half past 6:00
○ 6:30
● half past 8:00

14. Which shapes are curved? Choose all that apply.

● ○
○ △
● ○ (square)
● ○ (small circle)

15. Write each addition sentence in the box that shows the sum.

1 + 5   4 + 0   3 + 2   0 + 4   5 + 1

4	5	6
0 + 4	3 + 2	5 + 1
4 + 0		1 + 5

19. Write a number to make the sentence true.

2 + 10 = 7 + 5

Use the tally chart to answer questions 20 and 21.

Our Favorite Lunch		Total
pizza		8
salad	𝍸	
spaghetti	III	

20. How many children chose salad?

5

21. Circle the words that make the sentence true.

The number of tally marks for salad is (greater than) / less than / equal to the number of tally marks for spaghetti.

Answer: greater than (circled)

GO ON

22. Circle the number that makes the sentence true.

Ava has 7 white shirts, 3 blue shirts, and 5 gray shirts. How many shirts does Ava have in all?

Ava has [13 / (15) / 18] shirts.

Answer: 15 (circled)

23. Match the models to the number sentences.

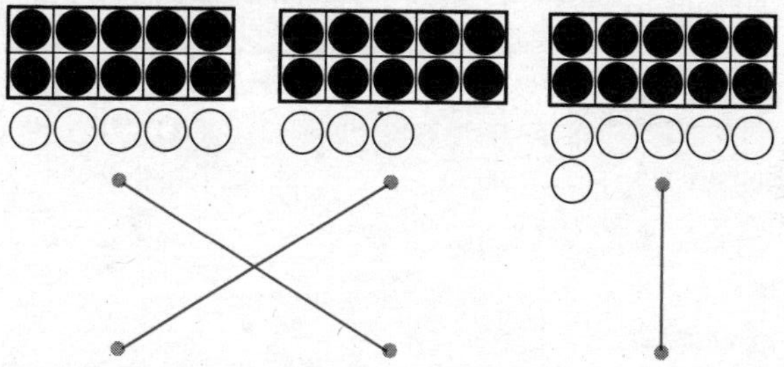

10 + 3 = 13 10 + 5 = 15 10 + 6 = 16

24. Compare. Is the math sentence true? Choose Yes or No.

37 is greater than 28.	● Yes	○ No
62 is greater than 64.	○ Yes	● No
38 > 44	○ Yes	● No
55 > 23	● Yes	○ No

STOP

Lola plays a game. There are 10 blocks. Lola throws a ball to knock over some of the blocks.

3. Draw a picture to show the blocks. Cross out the ones Lola knocks over. Write a subtraction sentence to show how many blocks are left.

Check children's work.

4. Lola knocks over the rest of the blocks one at a time. Write subtraction sentences to show how many blocks are left each time.

Check children's work.

At the Block Party

Jason, Kwame, and Lola go to a block party. There are balloons, games, pony rides, and snacks.

Jason gets 12 balloons. Some are green. Some are yellow.

1. Draw Jason's balloons. Write a number sentence about them.

Check children's work.

2. Jason gets 3 more green balloons. How many green balloons does he have now? How many balloons does he have in all? Write number sentences to tell how you know.

Check children's work.

_____ green balloons

_____ balloons in all

There are some kids waiting at the pony ride. The number of kids is more than 3 and fewer than 8.

5. Draw the kids waiting in line. Then, draw the same number of kids again to make a double.

Check children's drawings.

6. Write the addition sentence to show how many kids there are now.

Check children's work.

GO ON

Kwame goes to the snack stand. He gets 17 snacks. Some snacks are bananas. The rest are apples.

7. Draw pictures to show Kwame's snacks. Write how many bananas and apples he has.

Check children's drawings.

Possible answers are shown.

8 bananas   9 apples

Write a number sentence to tell how you know your answers are correct.

8 + 9 = 17

8. Write the related facts about Kwame's snacks.

Possible answers are shown.

9 + 8 = 17; 17 − 8 = 9; 17 − 9 = 8

STOP

At the Block Party

COMMON CORE STANDARDS

1.OA.1 Use addition and subtraction within 20 to solve word problems involving situations of adding to, taking from, putting together, taking apart, and comparing, with unknowns in all positions, e.g., by using objects, drawings, and equations with a symbol for the unknown number to represent the problem.

1.OA.3 Apply properties of operations as strategies to add and subtract.

1.OA.6 Add and subtract within 20, demonstrating fluency for addition and subtraction within 10. Use strategies such as counting on; making ten; decomposing a number leading to a ten; using the relationship between addition and subtraction; and creating equivalent but easier or known sums.

1.OA.8 Determine the unknown whole number in an addition or subtraction equation relating three whole numbers.

PURPOSE

To assess the ability to model and write number sentences to represent taking apart and putting together numbers within 20, to apply strategies to add and subtract within 20, and to identify and record related addition and subtraction facts within 20

TIME

40–45 minutes

GROUPING

Individuals

MATERIALS

- Performance Task, paper, pencil
- Two-color counters and ten frames (optional)

PREPARATION HINTS

- Review together taking apart and putting together numbers with children before assigning the task.
- Review writing addition and subtraction sentences with children before assigning the task.
- Review vocabulary, including *subtraction sentence*, *addition sentence*, and *related facts*.

IMPLEMENTATION NOTES

- Read the task aloud to children and make sure that all children have a clear understanding of the task.
- Children may use manipulatives to complete the task.
- Allow children as much paper as they need to complete the task.
- Allow as much time as children need to complete the task.
- Children must complete the task individually, without collaboration.
- Collect all work when the task is complete.

TASK SUMMARY

Children use understanding of part-part-whole relationships to model "taking apart" and "putting together" numbers within 20. They represent these situations by writing addition and subtraction sentences. They use a variety of strategies to add and subtract including using doubles, making a 10, and using related facts.

REPRESENTATION

In this task teachers can…

- Provide options for language, mathematical expressions and symbols by reviewing vocabulary and symbols in the context of children's prior knowledge.
- Provide options for comprehension by using cues to draw attention to critical features.

ACTION and EXPRESSION

In this task teachers can…

- Provide options for physical action by offering counters and ten frames to children while completing the task.

ENGAGEMENT

In this task teachers can…

- Sustain effort and persistence by providing specific feedback.
- Provide options for self-assessment by offering strategies for checking work.

EXPECTED STUDENT OUTCOMES

- Complete the task within the time allowed
- Reflect engagement in a productive struggle
- Model and write equations to solve addition and subtraction problems within 20
- Use strategies such as doubles, making a 10, and related facts to add and subtract within 20

SCORING

Use the associated Rubric to evaluate each child's work.

Performance Task Rubric

AT THE BLOCK PARTY

A level 3 response	• Indicates that the child has made sense of the task and persevered
	• Accurately uses understanding of part-part-whole relationships to model situations of "taking apart" and "putting together"
	• Demonstrates understanding of using number sentences to represent addition and subtraction
	• Shows the ability to accurately apply a variety of strategies to add and subtract within 20
A level 2 response	• Indicates that the child has made sense of the task and persevered
	• Shows the ability to accurately use understanding of part-part-whole relationships to model situations of "taking apart" and "putting together"
	• Demonstrates understanding of using number sentences to represent addition and subtraction
	• Shows the ability to accurately apply a variety of strategies to add and subtract within 20
	• Addresses most or all aspects of the task, but there may be errors of omission
A level 1 response	• Shows that the child has made sense of at least some elements of the task
	• Shows evidence of understanding of how "taking apart" and "putting together" situations can be modeled
	• Demonstrates some understanding of using number sentences to represent addition and subtraction
	• May not indicate the ability to accurately apply strategies to add and subtract
A level 0 response	• Shows little evidence that the child has made sense of the problems of the task
	• Reflects a lack of understanding of how to model situations involving "taking apart" and "putting together"
	• Reflects a lack of understanding of how to use number sentences to represent addition and subtraction
	• Shows little evidence of addressing the elements of the task

4. Choose all the ways that show the same number.

5. Is the first line shorter than the second line?
Choose Yes or No.

● Yes   ○ No

● Yes   ○ No

○ Yes   ● No

6. Use mental math. Write the numbers that are
10 less and 10 more than the number shown.

| 5 | 15 | 25 |

---

1. Use the 🔗 below. About how
long is the 🐛 ?

about ___3___

2. Count back. Write the number that is 1 less.

5 – 1 = 4

3. Ellen built this shape.

Which objects did Ellen use?
Circle them.

Draw another way to combine the objects.

Check children's drawings.

---

7. Look at the number sentences. What number is missing? Write the number in each box.

$13 - \boxed{4} = 9$ $9 + \boxed{4} = 13$

8. Use the hundred chart to add. Count on by ones or tens.

1	2	3	4	5	6	7	8	9	10
11	12	13	14	15	16	17	18	19	20
21	22	23	24	25	26	27	28	29	30
31	32	33	34	35	36	37	38	39	40
41	42	43	44	45	46	47	48	49	50
51	52	53	54	55	56	57	58	59	60
61	62	63	64	65	66	67	68	69	70
71	72	73	74	75	76	77	78	79	80
81	82	83	84	85	86	87	88	89	90
91	92	93	94	95	96	97	98	99	100

$37 + 5 = \underline{42}$

Explain how you used the chart to find the sum.

Possible answer: I start at 37. I count on 5 ones.

9. Julia buys 12 books. She gives 9 books away. How many books does she have left?

12
9

$\underline{3}$ books left

---

10. Kayla made a pie. Color one half of the pie.

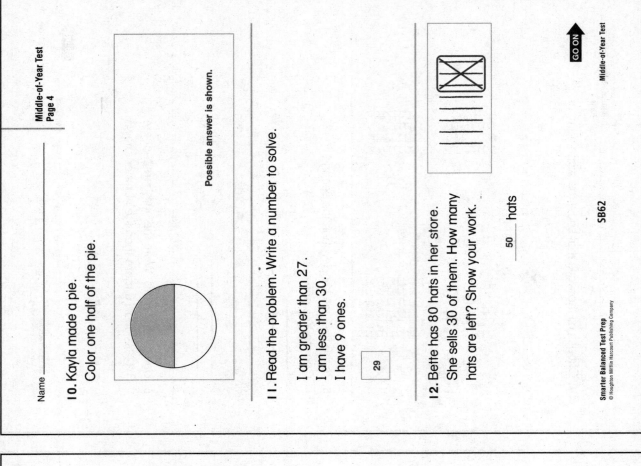

Possible answer is shown.

11. Read the problem. Write a number to solve.

I am greater than 27.
I am less than 30.
I have 9 ones.

$\boxed{29}$

12. Bette has 80 hats in her store. She sells 30 of them. How many hats are left? Show your work.

$\underline{50}$ hats

Name _____

13. Choose all the ways that name the time on the clock.

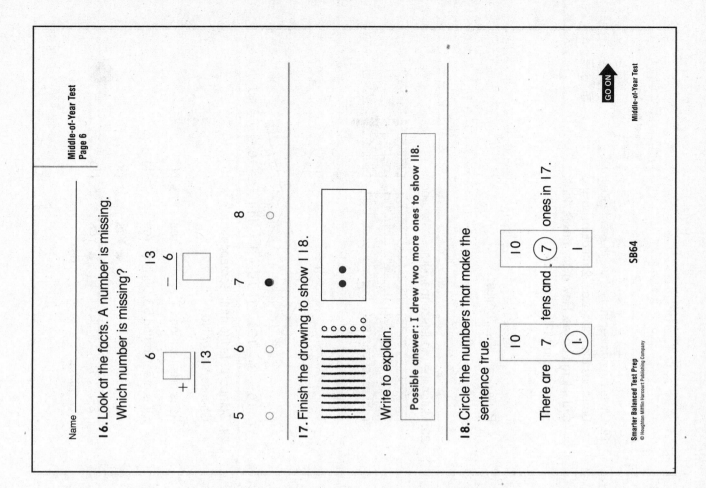

○ half past 6:00   ● half past 11:00

○ 6:00   ● 11:30

14. Which shapes have only 3 sides? Choose all that apply.

15. Write each addition sentence in the box that shows the sum.

$4+3$ $3+4$ $3+3$ $3+5$ $5+3$

6	7	8
$3+3$	$3+4$	$3+5$
	$4+3$	$5+3$

SB63

Name _____

16. Look at the facts. A number is missing. Which number is missing?

$6 + \boxed{} = 13$

$13 - \boxed{} = 6$

○ 5   ● 6   ○ 7   ○ 8

17. Finish the drawing to show 118.

Write to explain.

Possible answer: I drew two more ones to show 118.

18. Circle the numbers that make the sentence true.

There are ① 7 10 tens and 7⃝ 10 ones in 17.

SB64

SB63-SB64

Answer Key

Write a number to make the sentence true.

19. ___9___ = 2 + 3 + 4

20. Yuki sees 3 🚗. She sees 2 more 🚗.
She sees 1 fewer 🚐 than 🚐.
Graph the data.

What Yuki Sees

🚗 car						
🚚 truck						
🚐 van						
	0	1	2	3	4	5	6

21. Use Yuki's graph to answer the question.

How many 🚗 does Yuki see?

5

---

22. Circle the number that makes the sentence true.
Boris has 8 small boxes, 2 medium boxes,
and 4 large boxes. How many boxes does
Boris have in all?

Boris has
⟨14⟩ boxes.
16
17

23. Match the models to the number sentences.

10 + 3 = 13   10 + 1 = 11   10 + 0 = 10

24. Compare. Is the math sentence true?
Choose Yes or No.

	Yes	No
49 is greater than 57.	○ Yes	● No
54 is greater than 53.	● Yes	○ No
60 > 50	● Yes	○ No
72 > 68	● Yes	○ No

Lucy's Craft Store

Lucy has a craft store.

At the store children do projects with beads, stickers, buttons, and clay.

Today many children are in the store making projects.

Janey makes a necklace with beads.
Beads come in packs of 10.
She needs more than 40 beads.
She needs less than 50 beads.

1. Write a number of beads Janey can use. Draw packs of beads and single beads to show the number. Write how many tens and ones.

Possible response is shown. Check children's drawings.

46; 4 tens 6 ones

10 beads

---

2. Show the same number of beads in a different way. Use pictures, words, and numbers.

Check children's work.

3. Janey adds another pack of 10 beads. Write the number of beads Janey has now.

Check children's work.

Meg, Kira, and Juan put stickers on a poster. Stickers come in packs of 10. The chart shows the stickers they use.

Meg	Kira	Juan
45	72	56

4. Write a number that is greater than Meg's stickers. Draw a quick picture to show your work. Write two sentences to compare the numbers. Use words or symbols.

   Check children's work.

5. Write a number that is less than Kira's stickers. Draw a quick picture to show your work. Write two sentences to compare the numbers. Use words or symbols.

   Check children's work.

**Ned uses buttons to make puppets.
He has 38 round buttons.
He has 7 square buttons.**

6. Write an addition sentence to show how many buttons Ned has in all. Use pictures, words, and numbers.

   $38 + 7 = 45$

**Wendy uses clay to make animals.
Wendy has 6 packs of clay sticks.
Each pack has 10 sticks.
She uses 2 of her packs to make the animals.**

7. Write a subtraction sentence to show how many clay sticks Wendy has left. Use pictures, words, and numbers.

   $60 - 20 = 40$

8. Wendy gets 18 more sticks of clay. Write an addition sentence to show how many clay sticks Wendy has now. Use pictures, words, and numbers.

   $40 + 18 = 48$

Lucy's Craft Store

COMMON CORE STANDARDS

1.NBT.1 Count to 120, starting at any number less than 120. In this range, read and write numerals and represent a number of objects with a written numeral.

1.NBT.2 Understand that the two digits of a two-digit number represent amounts of tens and ones.

1.NBT.3 Compare two two-digit numbers based on meanings of the tens and ones digits, recording the results of comparisons with the symbols >, =, and <.

1.NBT.4 Add within 100, including adding a two-digit number and a one-digit number, and adding a two-digit number and a multiple of 10, using concrete models or drawings and strategies based on place value, properties of operations, and/or the relationship between addition and subtraction; relate the strategy to a written method and explain the reasoning used. Understand that in adding two-digit numbers, one adds tens and tens, ones and ones; and sometimes it is necessary to compose a ten.

PURPOSE

To assess the ability to model, read, and write numbers to 120; to use place value to compare numbers; to add and subtract 2-digit numbers

TIME

40–45 minutes

GROUPING

Individuals

MATERIALS

- Performance Task, paper, pencil
- Base-ten blocks (optional)

PREPARATION HINTS

- Review making groups of ten with children before assigning the task.
- Review equal groups, more, and fewer with children before assigning the task.
- Review basic addition and subtraction facts with children before assigning the task.
- Review vocabulary, including *digit, tens, ones, hundred, greater than, less than*.

IMPLEMENTATION NOTES

- Read the task aloud to children and make sure that all children have a clear understanding of the task.
- Children may use manipulatives to complete the task.
- Allow children as much paper as they need to complete the task.
- Allow as much time as children need to complete the task.
- Children must complete the task individually, without collaboration.
- Collect all children's work when the task is complete.

TASK SUMMARY

Children read, write, and model numbers using concepts of place value. They compare numbers using place value and the symbols greater than (>) and less than (<). They use place value concepts to add and subtract two-digit numbers including tens and tens and ones.

REPRESENTATION

In this task teachers can...

- Provide options for language, mathematical expressions and symbols by reviewing vocabulary and symbols in the context of students' prior knowledge.
- Clarify vocabulary by using word cards and matching numerals or symbols.

ACTION and EXPRESSION

In this task teachers can...

- Provide options for physical action by offering base-ten blocks to students while completing the task.

ENGAGEMENT

In this task, teachers can...

- Recruit interest by providing tasks that allow for active participation, exploration, and experimentation.
- Increase mastery by providing feedback that models identifying patterns of errors and wrong answers.

EXPECTED STUDENT OUTCOMES

- Complete the task within the time allowed
- Reflect engagement in a productive struggle
- Read, write, and model two-digit numbers
- Compare two-digit numbers using symbols
- Add and subtract two-digit numbers

SCORING

Use the associated Rubric to evaluate each child's work.

Performance Task Rubric

LUCY'S CRAFT STORE

A level 3 response	• Indicates that the child has made sense of the task and persevered • Demonstrates an understanding of place value as numbers that can be represented as tens and ones • Shows the ability to accurately apply place-value concepts when comparing numbers • Indicates an understanding of place-value concepts when adding 1- and 2-digit numbers, and subtracting multiples of tens
A level 2 response	• Indicates that the child has made sense of the task and persevered • Demonstrates an understanding of place value as numbers that can be represented as tens and ones • Shows the ability to accurately apply place-value concepts when comparing numbers • Indicates an understanding of place-value concepts when adding 1- and 2-digit numbers and subtracting of multiples of tens • Addresses most or all aspects of the task, but there may be errors of omission
A level 1 response	• Shows that the child has made sense of at least some elements of the task • Shows evidence of understanding that numbers are grouped as tens and ones • Demonstrates some understanding of comparing numbers • May not indicate an understanding of place value concepts when adding or subtracting 2-digit numbers
A level 0 response	• Shows little evidence that the child has made sense of the task • Reflects lack of understanding of place-value concepts in comparing numbers and adding or subtracting tens and ones • Shows little evidence of addressing the elements of the task

4. Choose all the ways that show the same number.

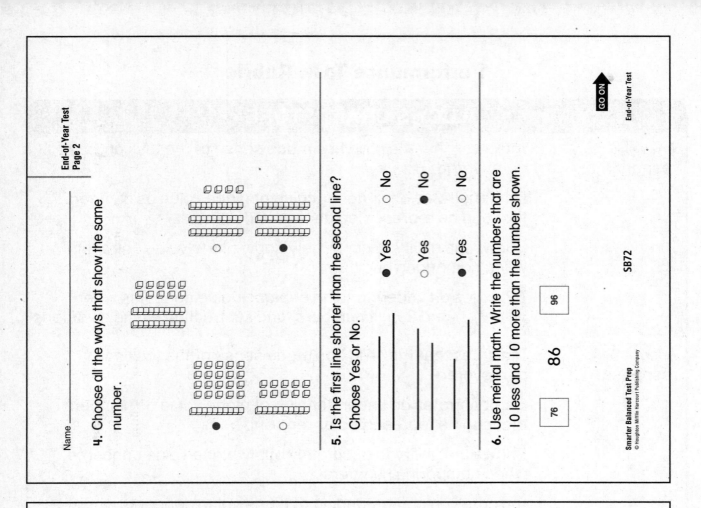

5. Is the first line shorter than the second line? Choose Yes or No.

● Yes   ○ No

○ Yes   ● No

● Yes   ○ No

6. Use mental math. Write the numbers that are 10 less and 10 more than the number shown.

| 76 | 86 | 96 |

1. Use the ⬭. How long is the pen?

about ___5___

2. Count back. Write the number that is 2 less.

$5 - 2 =$ | 3 |

3. José built this shape.

Which objects did José use? Circle them.

Draw another way to combine the objects.

Check children's drawings.

7. Look at the number sentences. What number is missing? Write the number in each box.

$14 - \boxed{6} = 8$ $\qquad$ $8 + \boxed{6} = 14$

8. Use the hundred chart to add. Count on by ones or tens.

$37 + 30 = \underline{67}$

1	2	3	4	5	6	7	8	9	10
11	12	13	14	15	16	17	18	19	20
21	22	23	24	25	26	27	28	29	30
31	32	33	34	35	36	37	38	39	40
41	42	43	44	45	46	47	48	49	50
51	52	53	54	55	56	57	58	59	60
61	62	63	64	65	66	67	68	69	70
71	72	73	74	75	76	77	78	79	80
81	82	83	84	85	86	87	88	89	90
91	92	93	94	95	96	97	98	99	100

Explain how you used the chart to find the sum.

Possible answer: I start at 37. I count on 3 tens.

9. Andy has 12 stickers. He gives 3 away. How many does he have left?

12	
3	9

__9__ stickers left

---

10. Sid made a pizza.
Color one fourth of the pizza.

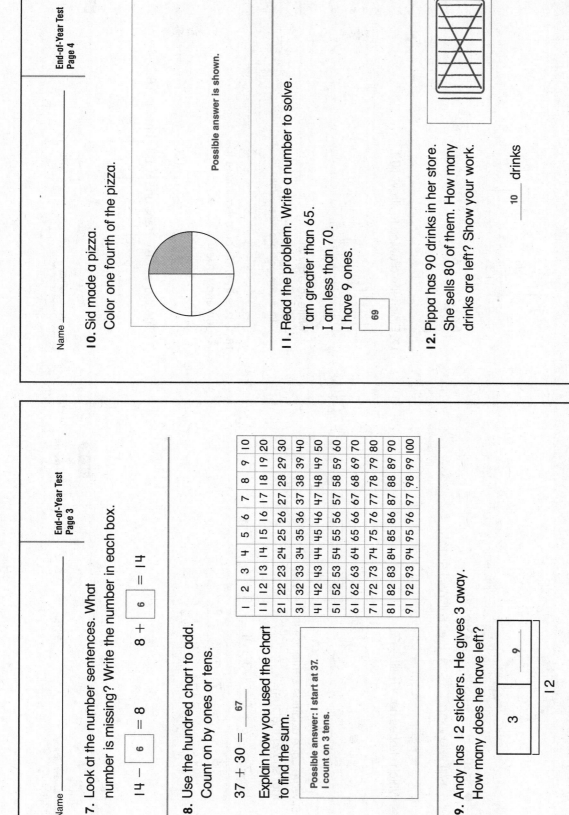

Possible answer is shown.

11. Read the problem. Write a number to solve.

I am greater than 65.
I am less than 70.
I have 9 ones.

$\boxed{69}$

12. Pippa has 90 drinks in her store. She sells 80 of them. How many drinks are left? Show your work.

__10__ drinks

13. Choose all the ways that name the time on the clock.

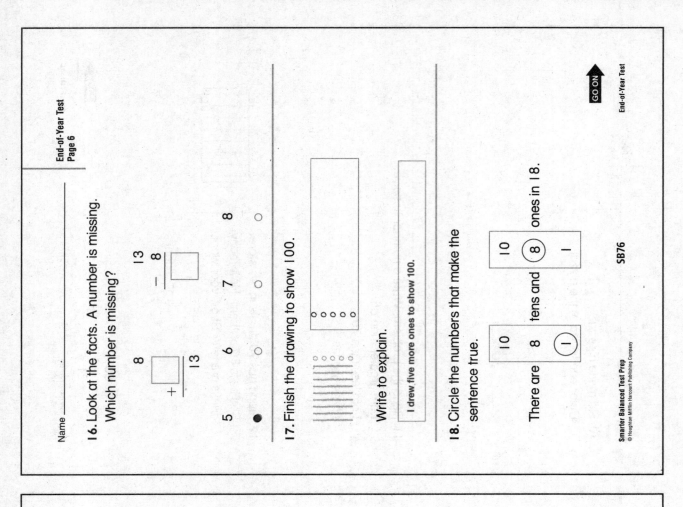

- ● 5:30
- ○ 6:30
- ○ half past 6:00
- ● half past 5:00

---

14. Which shapes have 4 sides?

○   ●   ○   ● □   ○ △   ● ▭

---

15. Write each addition sentence in the box that shows the sum.

1 + 7   6 + 0   3 + 4   0 + 6   7 + 1

6	7	8
0 + 6	3 + 4	1 + 7
6 + 0		7 + 1

GO ON
End-of-Year Test

---

16. Look at the facts. A number is missing. Which number is missing?

8
+ □
13

13
− 8
□

- ● 5
- ○ 6   ○ 7   ○ 8

---

17. Finish the drawing to show 100.

Write to explain.

I drew five more ones to show 100.

---

18. Circle the numbers that make the sentence true.

There are 8 tens and (8) ones in 18.

| (1) | 8 | 10 |

| 1 | (8) | 10 |

GO ON
End-of-Year Test

Name _____

Write a number to make the sentence true.

19. __6__ + 7 = 7 + 6

Use the bar graph to answer questions 20 and 21.

20. Compare ◊ and ☀ days. Circle the number that makes the sentence true.

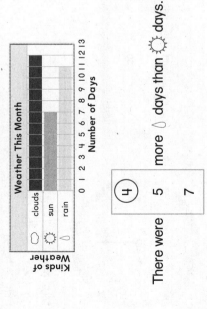

Weather This Month

Kinds of Weather: clouds, sun, rain

Number of Days: 0 1 2 3 4 5 6 7 8 9 10 11 12 13

There were [(4) 5 7] more ◊ days than ☀ days.

21. Ann says the graph shows 1 more rainy day than cloudy days. Is she correct?

Choose Yes or No.   ○ Yes   ● No

Explain your answer.

Possible answer: There was 1 more cloudy day than rainy days.

Name _____

22. Circle the number that makes the sentence true. Liam has 6 green marbles, 5 blue marbles, and 7 black marbles. How many marbles does he have in all?

Liam has [14 17 (18)] marbles.

23. Match the models to the number sentences.

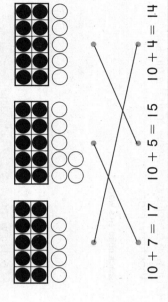

10 + 7 = 17   10 + 5 = 15   10 + 4 = 14

24. Compare. Is the math sentence true? Choose Yes or No.

45 is greater than 39.	● Yes	○ No
56 is greater than 58.	○ Yes	● No
74 > 66	● Yes	○ No
23 > 21	● Yes	○ No

Max Takes Measurements

**Max is telling time and comparing things.
Help Max take measurements and
record data.**

1. Max draws an hour hand pointing between
9 and 10 on the clock. Then he draws a
minute hand on the 6. Draw Max's clock.
Write the time.

9:30

2. Max draws an hour hand pointing to the
number 3 on the clock. Then he draws a
minute hand on the 12. Draw Max's clock.
Write the time.

3:00

**Max uses ⬭ to measure things.
Use ⬭.
Draw the things that Max measures.**

3. Draw a marker that is about 5 ⬭ long.

Check children's work.

4. Draw a pencil that is longer than the marker.
About how many ⬭ long is it?

Check children's work.

5. Draw a crayon that is shorter than the marker.
About how many ⬭ long is it?

Check children's work.

6. Write the names of the three objects in order
from shortest to longest.

Check children's work.

Max asked 18 kids which day they like best: Friday, Saturday, or Sunday. Nine children chose Saturday. Three children chose Sunday. The rest of the children chose Friday.

7. Make a tally chart to show the children's choices.

FAVORITE DAY		Total
Friday	卌 I	6
Saturday	卌 IIII	9
Sunday	III	3

Now use the tally chart to answer the questions.

8. How many children chose Friday? __6__

9. How many more children chose Saturday than Sunday? __6__

10. How many children chose Friday and Sunday in all? __9__

Fourteen kids in Max's class each have one pet. Max makes a bar graph to show each pet and the number of kids who have it. Seven kids have a dog. Four have a cat. Three have a fish.

11. Complete Max's bar graph.

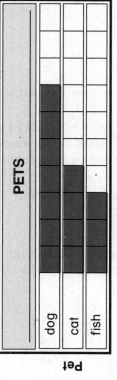

PETS

Pet — dog, cat, fish

Number of Children

Now use the graph to answer the questions.

12. Which pet do the most children have? __dog__

13. Which pet do the least children have? __fish__

14. How many dogs and fish in all do the children have? __10__

15. How many more children have a dog than a cat? __3__

Max Takes Measurements

COMMON CORE STANDARDS

1.MD.1   Order three objects by length; compare the lengths of two objects indirectly by using a third object.

1.MD.2   Express the length of an object as a whole number of length units, by laying multiple copies of a shorter object (the length unit) end to end; understand that the length measurement of an object is the number of same-size length units that span it with no gaps or overlaps.

1.MD.3   Tell and write time in hours and half-hours using analog and digital clocks.

PURPOSE

To assess the ability to use nonstandard units of measurement to compare and order length, to tell time to the hour and half hour using analog and digital clocks, and to read and make bar graphs and tally charts

TIME

40–45 minutes

GROUPING

Individuals

MATERIALS

- Performance Task, paper, pencil
- Crayons
- Paper clips

PREPARATION HINTS

- Review counting and ordering numbers with children before assigning the task.
- Review comparing length of objects with children before assigning the task.
- Review making and reading tally charts and bar graphs with children before assigning the task.

IMPLEMENTATION NOTES

- Read the task aloud to children and make sure that all children have a clear understanding of the task.
- Children may use manipulatives to complete the task.
- Allow children as much paper as they need to complete the task.
- Allow as much time as children need to complete the task.
- Children must complete the task individually, without collaboration.
- Collect all work when the task is complete.

TASK SUMMARY

Children draw clock hands and interpret the time. They draw objects, measure length, and compare length using a nonstandard measurement. They derive data and record the data in a tally chart or bar graph. They analyze and compare the data from the tally chart or bar graph.

REPRESENTATION

In this task teachers can…

- Provide options for language, mathematical expressions, and symbols by giving children multiple ways to represent time, to measure length, and to record data in a chart or graph.

ACTION and EXPRESSION

In this task teachers can…

- Provide options for physical action by having children draw clock hands, objects of defined lengths, bar graphs, and tally charts.

ENGAGEMENT

In this task, teachers can…

- Provide options for engagement by giving children individual choice and autonomy in choosing clock times, objects to draw, and data sets that fit the clues provided.

EXPECTED STUDENT OUTCOMES

- Complete the task within the time allowed
- Reflect engagement in a productive struggle
- Tell time to the half hour and hour in analog and digital
- Understand how to use a nonstandard unit of measurement
- Understand how to compare relative sizes of objects
- Make tally charts and bar graphs from data
- Read bar graphs and tally charts to analyze and compare data

SCORING

Use the associated Rubric to evaluate each child's work.

Performance Task Rubric

MAX TAKES MEASUREMENTS

A level 3 response	• Indicates that the child has made sense of the task and persevered
	• Demonstrates an understanding of how to tell and write time to the hour and half hour on analog and digital clocks
	• Shows an ability to compare objects based on relative size or on measurement in nonstandard units
	• Indicates an understanding of how to record, analyze, and compare data in a tally chart or bar graph
A level 2 response	• Indicates that the child has made sense of the task and persevered
	• Demonstrates an understanding of how to tell and write time to the hour and half hour on analog and digital clocks
	• Shows an ability to compare objects based on relative size or on measurement in nonstandard units
	• Indicates an understanding of how to record, analyze, and compare data in a tally chart or bar graph
	• Addresses most or all aspects of the task, but there may be errors of omission
A level 1 response	• Shows that the child has made sense of at least some elements of the task
	• Shows evidence of understanding of how to tell and write time
	• Demonstrates some understanding of how to use nonstandard units or compare relative sizes of objects
	• May reflect a lack of understanding of how to record, analyze, and compare data in a tally chart or bar graph
A level 0 response	• Shows little evidence that the child has made sense of the problems of the task
	• Reflects a lack of understanding of how to tell and write time
	• Reflects a lack of understanding of how to use nonstandard units or compare relative sizes of objects
	• Reflects a lack of understanding of how to use tally charts and bar graphs
	• Shows little evidence of addressing the elements of the task

The Fruit Market

Evan and April go to the fruit market.
They each pick out some fruit to share.

April buys 8 apples.
Some are red.
The rest are green.

I. Draw April's apples. Write an addition
sentence about them.

Check children's work.

_____ + _____ = 8

2. Write a related addition fact about April's apples.

Check children's work.

_____ + _____ = _____

GO ON ➡

3. Evan buys some oranges. He gives 1, 2, or 3 oranges to April. He has 5 oranges left. Draw pictures and write a number sentence to show how many oranges Evan could have bought.

Check children's work.

4. Evan gives 2 more oranges to friends. How many does he have left now? Write the addition fact that helps you subtract.

Check children's work.

Pablo buys between 11 and 19 peaches.

5. Draw to show a number of peaches
Pablo could buy. Circle to show tens
and ones in the drawing.

Check children's drawings.

---

6. Draw 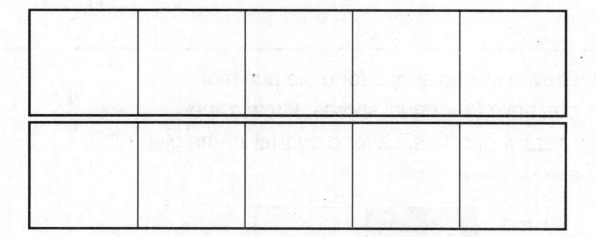 to show the number of peaches
in another way.   **Check children's drawings.**

---

7. Write how many tens and ones.

_____ tens   _____ ones

**Check that children's answers are
consistent with their drawings.**

Write the number of peaches. _____

GO ON ➡

Pablo bakes the peaches into pies that he can share with friends.

8. Draw a closed shape for a pie pan that can have two equal shares. Draw a line to show halves. Color half of the pie.

Possible answer is shown.

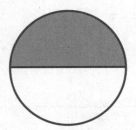

---

9. Draw a closed shape for a pie pan that can have four equal shares. Draw a line to show quarters. Color a quarter of the pie.

Possible answer is shown.

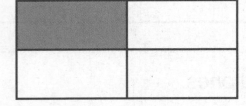

The Fruit Market

COMMON CORE STANDARDS

1.OA.1 Use addition and subtraction within 20 to solve word problems involving situations of adding to, taking from, putting together, taking apart, and comparing, with unknowns in all positions, e.g., by using objects, drawings, and equations with a symbol for the unknown number to represent the problem.

1.OA.3 Apply properties of operations as strategies to add and subtract. *Examples: If 8 + 3 = 11 is known, then 3 + 8 = 11 is also known. (Commutative property of addition.) To add 2 + 6 + 4, the second two numbers can be added to make a ten, so 2 + 6 + 4 = 2 + 10 = 12. (Associative property of addition.)*

1.OA.4 Understand subtraction as an unknown-addend problem.

1.OA.6 Add and subtract within 20, demonstrating fluency for addition and subtraction within 10. Use strategies such as counting on; making ten (e.g., 8 + 6 = 8 + 2 + 4 = 10 + 4 = 14); decomposing a number leading to a ten (e.g., 13 − 4 = 13 − 3 − 1 = 10 − 1 = 9); using the relationship between addition and subtraction (e.g., knowing that 8 + 4 = 12, one knows 12 − 8 = 4); and creating equivalent but easier or known sums (e.g., adding 6 + 7 by creating the known equivalent 6 + 6 + 1 = 12 + 1 = 13).

1.NBT.2b The numbers from 11 to 19 are composed of a ten and one, two, three, four, five, six, seven, eight, or nine ones.

1.G.3 Partition circles and rectangles into two and four equal shares, describe the shares using the words *halves*, *fourths*, and *quarters*, and use the phrases *half of*, *fourth of*, and *quarter of*. Describe the whole as two of, or four of the shares. Understand for these examples that decomposing into more equal shares creates smaller shares.

PURPOSE

To assess the ability to solve addition and subtraction word problems

To assess the ability to represent 11–19 as tens and ones

To assess the ability to partition shapes into two and four equal shares

TIME

40–45 minutes

GROUPING

Individuals

MATERIALS

- Performance Task, paper, pencil
- Connecting cubes (optional)

PREPARATION HINTS

- Review that a "ten" is a group of ten ones.
- Review the vocabulary *equal share*, *halves*, and *fourths*.

IMPLEMENTATION NOTES

- Read the task aloud to children and make sure that all children have a clear understanding of the task.
- Children may use manipulatives to complete the task.
- Allow children as much paper as they need to complete the task.
- Allow as much time as children need to complete the task.
- Children must complete the task individually, without collaboration.
- Collect all work when the task is complete.

TASK SUMMARY

Children use strategies to solve addition and subtraction word problems. They use drawings and numerals to represent 11–19 as tens and ones. They also partition shapes into two and four equal shares to show halves and fourths.

REPRESENTATION

In this task teachers can…

- Provide options for comprehension by reviewing how to use a ten frame.
- Guide children to visualize problems by picturing scenarios in their minds.

ACTION and EXPRESSION

In this task teachers can…

- Provide options for physical action by having children act out the addition and subtraction problems with objects such as connecting cubes.

ENGAGEMENT

In this task teachers can…

- Optimize relevance by having children talk about their own experiences like the ones on the task.
- Provide options for self-assessment by offering strategies for checking work.

EXPECTED STUDENT OUTCOMES

- Complete the task within the time allowed
- Reflect engagement in a productive struggle
- Solve addition and subtraction word problems
- Represent 11–19 as tens and ones
- Partition shapes into two and four equal shares

SCORING

Use the associated Rubric to evaluate each child's work.

Year-End Performance Assessment Task Rubric

THE FRUIT MARKET

A level 3 response	• Indicates that the child has made sense of the task and persevered
	• Demonstrates understanding of addition and subtraction, and place value
	• Shows the ability to partition shapes into equal shares
A level 2 response	• Indicates that the child has made sense of the task and persevered
	• Demonstrates understanding of addition and subtraction, and place value
	• Shows the ability to partition shapes into equal shares
	• Addresses most or all aspects of the task, but there may be errors of omission
A level 1 response	• Shows that the child has made sense of at least some elements of the task
	• Demonstrates little understanding of addition and subtraction, and place value
	• May not show the ability to partition shapes into equal shares
	• Addresses some aspects of the task, but there may be some procedural or computational errors
A level 0 response	• Shows little evidence that the child has made sense of the problems of the task
	• Reflects lack of understanding of addition and subtraction, and place value
	• Reflects lack of understanding of how to partition shapes into equal shares
	• Shows little evidence of addressing the elements of the task

Intervention Resources

		Soar to Success: Math	Response to Intervention
Domain: Operations and Algebraic Thinking			
Represent and solve problems involving addition and subtraction.			
1.OA.1	Use addition and subtraction within 20 to solve word problems involving situations of adding to, taking from, putting together, taking apart, and comparing, with unknowns in all positions, e.g., by using objects, drawings, and equations with a symbol for the unknown number to represent the problem.	Warm-Up: 10.03, 10.09, 10.13, 11.03, 11.04. 11.07, 11.11, 29.33, 60.02, 66.01,	Tier 1 Lessons: 1–14 Tier 2/3 Skills and Activities: 3, 5, 10, 11, 12, 13, 17, 22, 23, 24, 25, 26, 38, 39, 40, 41, 43, 44, 46, 47
1.OA.2	Solve word problems that call for addition of three whole numbers whose sum is less than or equal to 20, e.g., by using objects, drawings, and equations with a symbol for the unknown number to represent the problem.	Warm-Up: 10.05	Tier 1 Lessons: 15 Tier 2/3 Skills and Activities: 27, 28, 31, 37
Understand and apply properties of operations and the relationship between addition and subtraction.			
1.OA.3	Apply properties of operations as strategies to add and subtract. *Examples: If 8 + 3 = 11 is known, then 3 + 8 = 11 is also known. (Commutative property of addition.) To add 2 + 6 + 4, the second two numbers can be added to make a ten, so 2 + 6 + 4 = 2 + 10 = 12. (Associative property of addition.)*	Warm-Up: 10.08, 10.18, 10.19, 10.20, 10.24	Tier 1 Lessons: 16–20 Tier 2/3 Skills and Activities: 8, 12, 24, 27, 28, 31
1.OA.4	Understand subtraction as an unknown-addend problem.	Warm-Up: 29.21	Tier 1 Lessons: 21, 22 Tier 2/3 Skills and Activities: 12
Add and subtract within 20.			
1.OA.5	Relate counting to addition and subtraction (e.g., by counting on 2 to add 2).	Warm-Up: 10.02, 11.13	Tier 1 Lessons: 23, 24 Tier 2/3 Skills and Activities: 16, 29
1.OA.6	Add and subtract within 20, demonstrating fluency for addition and subtraction within 10. Use strategies such as counting on; making ten (e.g., 8 + 6 = 8 + 2 + 4 = 10 + 4 = 14); decomposing a number leading to a ten (e.g., 13 − 4 = 13 − 3 − 1 = 10 − 1 = 9); using the relationship between addition and subtraction (e.g., knowing that 8 + 4 = 12, one knows 12 − 8 = 4); and creating equivalent but easier or known sums (e.g., adding 6 + 7 by creating the known equivalent 6 + 6 + 1 = 12 + 1 = 13).	Warm-Up: 1.12, 10.02, 10.04, 10.11, 10.12, 10.17, 10.21, 10.20, 11.03, 11.10, 11.15, 29.21, 29.29, 29.30, 29.31, 29.32	Tier 1 Lessons: 25–41 Tier 2/3 Skills and Activities: 4, 6, 12, 15, 17, 24, 28, 29, 30, 32, 33, 35, 36, 42, 45, 49, 50, 51, 53
Work with addition and subtraction equations.			
1.OA.7	Understand the meaning of the equal sign, and determine if equations involving addition and subtraction are true or false. For example, which of the following equations are true and which are false? 6 = 6, 7 = 8 − 1, 5 + 2 = 2 + 5, 4 + 1 = 5 + 2.		Tier 1 Lessons: 42 Tier 2/3 Skills and Activities: 24, 42
1.OA.8	Determine the unknown whole number in an addition or subtraction equation relating three whole numbers.	Warm-Up: 11.06, 11.11, 29.23	Tier 1 Lessons: 43-46 Tier 2/3 Skills and Activities: 1, 3, 5, 9, 17, 24, 28, 42, 48, 52

Intervention Resources

		Soar to Success: Math	Response to Intervention
Domain: Number and Operations in Base Ten			
Extend the counting sequence.			
1.NBT.1	Count to 120, starting at any number less than 120. In this range, read and write numerals and represent a number of objects with a written numeral.	Warm-Up: 2.20, 28.12, 28.14,	Tier 1 Lessons: 47–50 Tier 2/3 Skills and Activities: 16, 17, 19, 56, 60
Understand place value.			
1.NBT.2	Understand that the two digits of a two-digit number represent amounts of tens and ones.	Warm-Up: 1.14, 1.15	Tier 1 Lessons: 51, 52 Tier 2/3 Skills and Activities: 56, 57
1.NBT.2a	10 can be thought of as a bundle of ten ones — called a "ten."	Warm-Up: 2.19	Tier 1 Lessons: 53 Tier 2/3 Skills and Activaities: 60, 68
1.NBT.2b	The numbers from 11 to 19 are composed of a ten and one, two, three, four, five, six, seven, eight, or nine ones.	Warm-Up: 1.13	Tier 1 Lessons: 54, 55 Tier 2/3 Skills and Activities: 54, 55
1.NBT.2c	The numbers 10, 20, 30, 40, 50, 60, 70, 80, 90 refer to one, two, three, four, five, six, seven, eight, or nine tens (and 0 ones).	Warm-Up: 1.16	Tier 1 Lessons: 56 Tier 2/3 Skills and Activities: 14
1.NBT.3	Compare two two-digit numbers based on meanings of the tens and ones digits, recording the results of comparisons with the symbols >, =, and <.	Warm-Up: 7.15, 7.17	Tier 1 Lessons: 57–60 Tier 2/3 Skills and Activities: 3, 5, 21, 59
Use place value understanding and properties of operations to add and subtract.			
1.NBT.4	Add within 100, including adding a two-digit number and a one-digit number, and adding a two-digit number and a multiple of 10, using concrete models or drawings and strategies based on place value, properties of operations, and/or the relationship between addition and subtraction; relate the strategy to a written method and explain the reasoning used. Understand that in adding two-digit numbers, one adds tens and tens, ones and ones; and sometimes it is necessary to compose a ten.	Warm-Up: 10.25, 10.28, 10.30	Tier 1 Lessons: 61–66 Tier 2/3 Skills and Activities: 18, 24, 29, 35, 54, 58, 60, 61, 63, 64, 65
1.NBT.5	Given a two-digit number, mentally find 10 more or 10 less than the number, without having to count; explain the reasoning used.	Warm-Up: 28.14	Tier 1 Lessons: 67 Tier 2/3 Skills and Activities: 19, 60, 61
1.NBT.6	Subtract multiples of 10 in the range 10–90 from multiples of 10 in the range 10–90 (positive or zero differences), using concrete models or drawings and strategies based on place value, properties of operations, and/or the relationship between addition and subtraction; relate the strategy to a written method and explain the reasoning used.	Warm-Up: 10.25, 10.28, 10.30, 11.18	Tier 1 Lessons: 68, 69 Tier 2/3 Skills and Activities: 34, 60, 62, 64, 65, 66, 67

Intervention Resources

		Soar to Success: Math	Response to Intervention
Domain: Measurement and Data			
Measure lengths indirectly and by iterating length units.			
1.MD.1	Order three objects by length; compare the lengths of two objects indirectly by using a third object.	Warm-Up: 41.02, 41.05	Tier 1 Lessons: 70, 71 Tier 2/3 Skills and Activities: 92, 93
1.MD.2	Express the length of an object as a whole number of length units, by laying multiple copies of a shorter object (the length unit) end to end; understand that the length measurement of an object is the number of same-size length units that span it with no gaps or overlaps. *Limit to contexts where the object being measured is spanned by a whole number of length units with no gaps or overlaps.*	Warm-Up: 41.06	Tier 1 Lessons: 72, 73, 74 Tier 2/3 Skills and Activities: 17, 94
Tell and write time.			
1.MD.3	Tell and write time in hours and half-hours using analog and digital clocks.	Warm-Up: 51.08, 51.10	Tier 1 Lessons: 75–78 Tier 2/3 Skills and Activities: 20, 95, 96, 97
Represent and interpret data.			
1.MD.4	Organize, represent, and interpret data with up to three categories; ask and answer questions about the total number of data points, how many in each category, and how many more or less are in one category than in another.	Warm-Up: 54.03, 54.04, 54.05, 54.06, 54.10	Tier 1 Lessons: 79–85 Tier 2/3 Skills and Activities: 2, 7, 21, 29, 37, 87, 88, 89, 90, 91
Domain: Geometry			
Reason with shapes and their attributes.			
1.G.1	Distinguish between defining attributes (e.g., triangles are closed and three-sided) versus non-defining attributes (e.g., color, orientation, overall size); build and draw shapes to possess defining attributes.	Warm-Up: 38.11, 38.12, 39.17, 39.26, 39.33	Tier 1 Lessons: 86–89 Tier 2/3 Skills and Activities: 69, 70, 71, 72, 73, 74, 75, 76, 77, 82, 84
1.G.2	Compose two-dimensional shapes (rectangles, squares, trapezoids, triangles, half-circles, and quarter-circles) or three-dimensional shapes (cubes, right rectangular prisms, right circular cones, and right circular cylinders) to create a composite shape, and compose new shapes from the composite shape.	Warm-Up: 38.17, 38.19, 39.26, 39.28	Tier 1 Lessons: 90–97 Tier 2/3 Skills and Activities: 71, 72, 73, 74, 75, 78, 79, 80, 82, 83, 85, 86
1.G.3	Partition circles and rectangles into two and four equal shares, describe the shares using the words *halves*, *fourths*, and *quarters*, and use the phrases *half of*, *fourth of*, and *quarter of*. Describe the whole as two of, or four of the shares. Understand for these examples that decomposing into more equal shares creates smaller shares.	Warm-Up: 5.03, 5.05	Tier 1 Lessons: 98, 99, 100 Tier 2/3 Skills and Activities: 81

Name _____

Student Record Form

Item	Common Core Standard	Beginning-of-Year	Middle-of-Year	End-of-Year
1	1.MD.2			
2	1.OA.5			
3	1.G.2			
4	1.NBT.2a			
5	1.MD.1			
6	1.NBT.5			
7	1.OA.8			
8	1.NBT.4			
9	1.OA.1			
10	1.G.3			
11	1.NBT.2c			
12	1.NBT.6			
13	1.MD.3			
14	1.G.1			
15	1.OA.3			
16	1.OA.4			
17	1.NBT.1			
18	1.NBT.2b			
19	1.OA.7			
20	1.MD.4			
21	1.MD.4			
22	1.OA.2			
23	1.OA.6			
24	1.NBT.3			

Class Record Form

Name of Student